A Guide to Educating Homeless Students

By

Jenna Tremayne

Introduction

This handbook was designed to assist teachers of homeless students in understanding what classrooms procedures can best influence the child. This book will define and address the following topics:

A.   Definitions and Background

B.   Attendance and Mobility

C.   Behavior Management

D.   Classroom Physical Environment

E.   Socialization

F.   Academic Assistance

G.   Parent Contact

H.   Community Support

Definitions

When many of us picture a homeless child, we imagine a young boy or girl who is dirty, cold, and sleeping on a street bench. Although, sadly, that may be true for a small amount of homeless children, homelessness involves much more. It is crucial for teachers to truly understand all we can about these children so we can better meet their specific needs. Homeless students can live in a variety of different places and may have different needs because of it. Take a minute and try to think of all the different places a child could live and still be identified as homeless (hint: there 6 definitions according to the McKinney-Vento Act).

The definition of homeless students is outlined in the McKinney-Vento Act and is summarized on the following page.

Homeless students can be:	Meaning	Classroom Effects
"Doubled-Up"	Living with other persons (usually family members or close friends) due to economic difficulty	-Student may not have a place of their own if living in a crowded place -Students may not rest enough if sleeping in places not made for rest -Students may lack health care and nutrition
In "Temporary Homes"	Living in motels, hotels, camp grounds due to economic hardships	-Students may be in unsafe motels -Students may be sharing a bed or sleeping on a cot and receive limited rest -Students may lack health care and nutrition
In Other Shelters	Emergency or Transitional Shelters or Half-Way Homes	-Students may not have a place of their own if the shelters are crowded -Students may not have quiet places to study or rest -Students may lack health care and nutrition
In Limbo	Have been abandoned at police stations, fire departments, hospitals, or are waiting to be placed in foster homes	-Students are often feeling abandoned, afraid, and unloved -Students may not have a quiet place to rest or do homework -Students may lack health care and nutrition
In Public	Live in public places not designed for sleeping or human habitation (parks, streets, benches, cars, abandoned buildings, bus stations, etc.)	-Students may express anger and fear due to living in unsafe public places -Students may show signs of frustration with authority -Students do not have a place of their own to keep their belongings -Students may lack health care and nutrition
On his/her own	Living without parents (runaways, or abandoned)	-Students may feel unloved and ignored -Students may show signs of frustration with authority -Students do not have a place of their own to keep their belongings -Students may lack health care and nutrition

Before We Begin...

You will need a lot of extra support once you become aware that you have a homeless student in your class. The people listed below are there to help you. Ask for their name, phone number (with extensions), e-mail addresses, and FAX numbers.

Make These People Your New Friends...

Position	Name	Phone	E-mail	FAX
District Homeless Liaison				
School Principal				
School/ District Nurse				
Local Shelter Director				
Local Food Bank Director				
County Counseling Center				
School Cafeteria				

Suggestion*- highlight the best way to reach the person so that it can help limit your waiting time for responses.

Attendance and Mobility

Attendance

As many teachers have experienced, it is very difficult to catch a student up on lessons when he/she is absent or consistently tardy. These behaviors are very common amongst homeless students and it is our job to understand why, and help prevent poor attendance.

Imagine a child's typical night. They eat dinner, shower, brush their teeth, (if they're lucky) listen to a bedtime story, and fall asleep in their bed. Now, imagine what health problems a child without a sink to brush his/her teeth in, without a shower daily, without a filling dinner, and without a warm bed. When homeless students are enrolled in schools it is often difficult for them to attend school daily because of medical problems. Many homeless children are exposed to more diseases than students who are not homeless and generally they do not have health care. As teachers, we can help our homeless students prevent diseases and thus improve attendance.

On the following page there is a list of books that can serve as fantastic resources, but as teachers it is our job to enforce these skills in class. Many school nurses will also come to classrooms and do demonstrations on hand washing, bathing, dental hygiene, and overall health tips. Reminding students to wash their hands (with warm water when available and for about 30 seconds or the length of the ABC song) when they're in the restroom, and before they eat lunch is crucial. Also, many homeless students may not have a place to wash their hands before a meal or brush their teeth before bed and in the morning. Ask your principal or school nurse if donations of hand sanitizer can be offered to the child or his/her guardian.

Here is a list of children and young adult books about cleanliness:

Germs Are Not For Sharing	Elizabeth Verdick ISBN: 1575421976	Reading Level: 1.6
Wash Your Hands	By: Tony Ross ISBN: 1929132018	Reading Level: 1.77
Sniffles, Sneezes, Hiccups, and Coughs	Penny Durant ISBN: 0756611075	Reading Level: 2.0
The Magic School Bus: A Book About Germs	Kate Eager ISBN: 0545034655	Reading Level: 2.6
Germs Make Me Sick	Melvin Berger ISBN: 9780064451543	Reading Level: 3.7
The Tooth Book: A Guide To Healthy Teeth and Gums	Edward Miller ISBN: 0823422062	Reading Level: 4.5
Germs (The Kidhaven Science Library Germs)	Don Nardo ISBN: 073770943X	Reading Level: 6.5

In addition to teaching overall hygiene, we can help provide students with the basic tools to ensure they are caring for their bodies as necessary. We can provide the student with a special place in the classroom that is just "theirs," and allow students to keep a plastic hygiene bag of floss, toothpaste and a toothbrush in this personalized spot (a drawer, a box in a cabinet, etc.) so the child can brush or floss on campus if necessary. The plastic bag should be hidden from other students view (such as in a lunch bag) as it is our job to keep all information confidential. Also, ask your district's homeless liaison or local business for donations of toothbrushes, floss, and toothpaste.

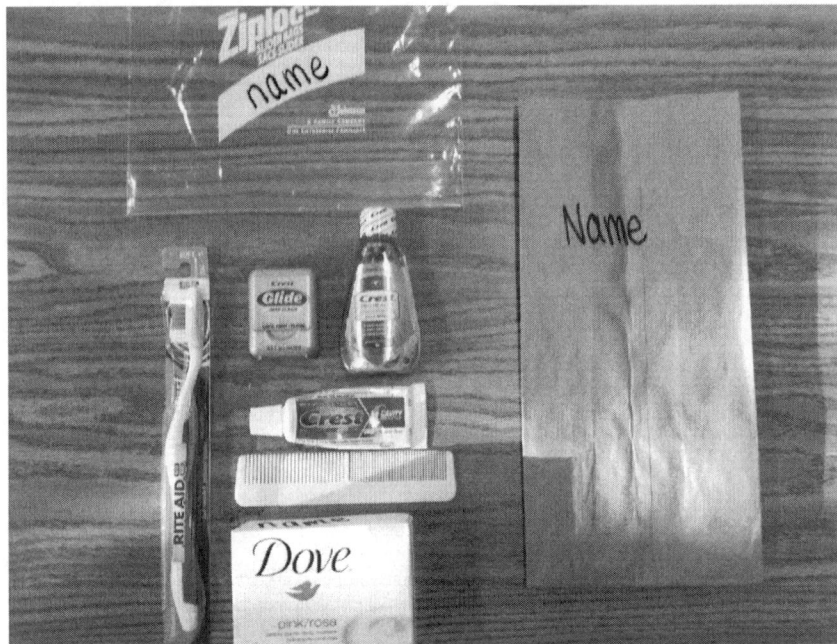

Mobility

Homeless students can often times be identified as "nomadic." Many homeless students and families move several times within a school year due to lack of affordable housing. Several shelters and halfway homes will offer temporary housing with a 30 to 90 day limit. Within these time constraints parents may be unable to find another place to stay in the area, students will then often move to new cities with other family members, friends, shelters, etc.

As teachers we know how long it can take for each school to receive the "Cumulative Files" and student records of new students, so it becomes our duty to assess students quickly and not only provide a copy for the students' portfolio but also to the student's guardians so that the data can quickly be transferred to the next teacher and school. Teachers should have a new student packet filled with assessments and new student information ready at all times because you never know when a new students may arrive in your classroom. Listed below is a checklist of items that should be in the new student packet:

1. A Self-Evaluation form (provided on the following page)
2. A reading and math assessment at current grade level and prior grade level
3. School Rules
4. School and class schedules

When we receive news that a student will no longer be attending our site, it is our duty to quickly assemble all the data we have so that it can be sent to the new school as quickly as possible. We should include:

☐ Most recent grades in all academic areas
☐ Behavior plans (if one was formed)
☐ Attendance records
☐ Photograph of the child and of the class
☐ Sample student work
☐ Reports of any diagnoses (learning disabilities, illnesses, etc.).
☐ A letter from the class to wish the student well in the student's new school
☐ A weekly evaluation form

*IF the student moves to another school, that school site will contact your office for student files. Contact the new school and teacher to inform the new teacher about the student's living situation and academic progress.

Self-Evaluation Form

Name _____ Date_____

Birthday _____ Age_____ Grade Level _____

1. The last time I attended school was
_____
_____

2. The last book I read was
_____

It was about _____

3. The last lesson I had in math was
_____
_____

4. My favorite subject in school is
_____
_____

5. In the past, I have had trouble in school with
_____
_____

6. How I feel about attending a new school is
_____
_____

7. Any important information I would like my teacher to know
_____
_____
_____
_____

Behavior Management

   Many of you may not have experienced homelessness. However you may be able to relate to how a homeless child feels with an experience of your own. Remember that day last week? The one where your alarm didn't go off you and you were almost late to work? The day you left your lunch on the kitchen counter and didn't bring cash to buy lunch in the cafeteria? Remember that same day; there was a fire drill and a PTA meeting to attend after work? That was a tough day wasn't it? You were hungry, tired, confused with a changing schedule, and not to mention grouchy! Yes, we've all had those days. But now, remember when you had those days as a child? Remember when mom would talk it over with you before bed or give you an ice cream cone to help cheer you up? Now imagine those tough days without mom's help and imagine being, let's say eight years old. Doesn't seem fun does it?

   Sadly, those types of days are constant for homeless students. Homeless students may not sleep in the same place (which may or may not be a bed) each night, they may not have a sack lunch, and may be very tired from a lack of nutrition and management. So, teachers, what do we see when any of us (adult, child, homebound, or homeless) are hungry and tired? Crankiness. That's right; we need to prepare ourselves for the moods, emotions, and fears of our homeless students.

   It is important to remember that when our homeless students start demonstrating unacceptable behaviors they are demonstrating a need. It could be a need of rest, food, safety, hope, or love. We can provide our students with each of these.

What to do when my homeless students are too tired?

When students are tired from a lack of sleep, arrange for a quiet spot in the classroom or in the nurses office where the student can rest for a short time (be sure to check with the school nurse first). Yes, they may miss a few minutes of a lesson, but they will return feeling renewed and more willing to listen and more capable of comprehension. The space in your classroom can be used by all students during silent reading or writing time as well, so don't think of it as "wasted space." You can even post writing or language posters near it for the times the space is used by others.

Students can (as a class if you choose) write about nights they sleep well or don't sleep well in their journals. Ask students to write about things they enjoy before bed and what types of things make them sleep better (they can draw pictures if primary). This will help you better understand why the child is exhausted. If the child is cold or lacks blankets or pillows you can ask for donations from your community (your school nurse and homeless liaison should be able to help you reach community organizations).

*In the picture you see, a rug, blankets, calming paintings, a writing station, and informative posters.

What to do when my homeless students are hungry?

Because it is challenging for our brain to function without the proper nourishments it needs, we need to be aware of our student's diets. If your homeless students are coming to school without breakfast or a packed lunch, immediately contact the school cafeteria for a free lunch application. Also, (remember to check for food allergies) provide the student with immediate nourishments kept in a safe, private place in the classroom.

Good snack choices include anything high in protein and not too high in sugars, such as: granola bars, trail mix, raisins, cheese and crackers, water bottles, etc. These can all be kept in your classroom year-round.

*Before purchasing items, see if your school can help pay for these snacks, or if the cafeteria has snacks available, if not, ask your local grocery store for donations, many managers are willing to give discounts or cover the cost completely.

Visit the following websites for more assistance:

http://feedingamerica.org/

http://www.foodpantries.org/

http://www.ampleharvest.org/find-pantry.php

http://www.homelessshelterdirectory.org/

How Do I Set-Up My Classroom?

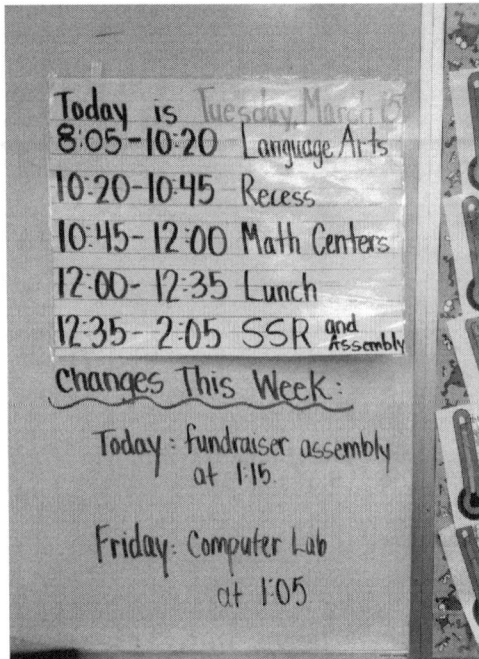

Today is Tuesday, March 15
8:05-10:20 Language Arts
10:20-10:45 Recess
10:45-12:00 Math Centers
12:00-12:35 Lunch
12:35-2:05 SSR and Assembly

Changes This Week:

Today: fundraiser assembly
at 1:15.

Friday: Computer Lab
at 1:05

Stay Consistent

Remind yourself that your classroom is the most consistent, safe place most homeless students are at in a day. Keep your class organized and predictable. Do not quickly change where you keep your pencils, it may confuse the homeless students. Keep your schedule consistent as well. Have a schedule posted, outlining the objectives of each lesson and the times. Keep to these times as much as possible. This will help relieve the students of anxiety and thus allow them to concentrate and learn more. If changes are to be made to the schedule, notify the students beforehand (as much as possible).

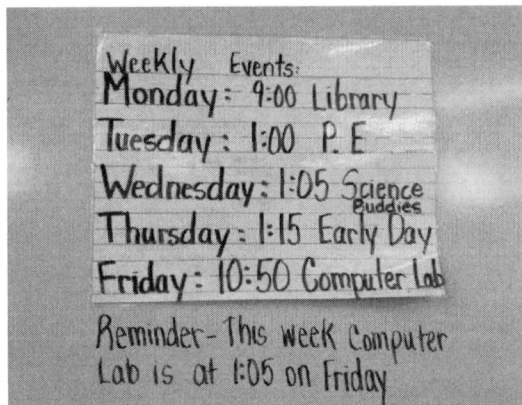

Weekly Events:
Monday: 9:00 Library
Tuesday: 1:00 P.E
Wednesday: 1:05 Science Buddies
Thursday: 1:15 Early Day
Friday: 10:50 Computer Lab

Reminder- This week Computer Lab is at 1:05 on Friday

POST as many dates/changes to the typical schedule as possible

What to do with the Unexpected Changes:

Fire Drills/Earthquake Drills:

Quietly whisper to the student that there will be a fire drill at ___ time. Explain that they will have the important job of getting the backpack, fire extinguisher, etc. Ask them to keep the secret so that it can seem as real as possible to all the other students. This will not take away the child's seriousness in the drill; in fact it will instill the child with responsibility.

Lock-Downs:

Call the student to your desk. Explain that we have been asked to stay inside for some extra time. Provide the student with a few minutes to write in his/her journal if this makes them feel uncomfortable. Try to keep the rest of the day as normal as possible.

Make The Room Student Accessible

Homeless students do not have the ability to open drawers or cabinets when looking for things within a house. The feeling like a place belongs to you is absent for these children. We can help provide students with a sense of belonging to a place by simply allowing students to have space in the classroom. Allow students to open drawers or cabinets to get out scissors, glue, paper, etc. when they need it. Students (even primary) do not need to have all items passed out to them. Students are more than capable of learning where items are and how to put them away properly.

Make a "Home-y" Environment

These students may have never seen a wreath, welcome mat, or hand towel. We can help them experience these common household items within the classroom. Here are some quick tips on how to help the student feel more at home in your classroom:

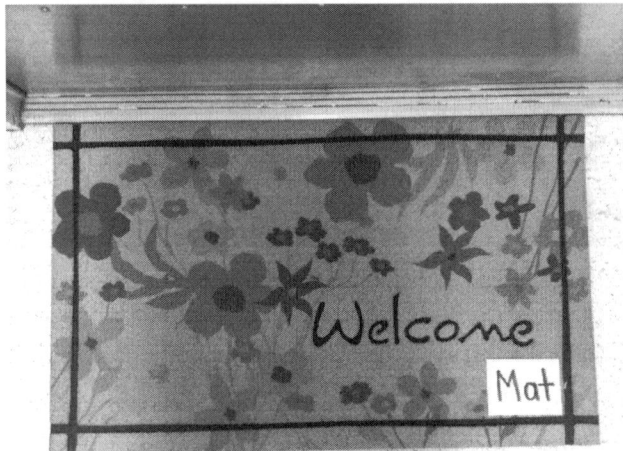

- ☐ Place a Welcome Mat at the door of the classroom
- ☐ If you have a sink, set a hand towel next to it
- ☐ Have a lighting that would generally be in a home such as a lamp
- ☐ Have area rugs on the floor (not ABC or academic rugs but home décor rugs)
- ☐ Set up picture frame of students (be sure to check permission before photographing)
- ☐ Have a couch, bean bag, or comfortable chair for quiet time
- ☐ Safe cleaning materials labeled such as: sponges, paper towels, soap, etc.

Socialization

Whole Group Instruction

Although school is for academic learning, it is no secret that a student's socialization is immensely important. Students need to have friends, learn to trust, and feel empathy and compassion. It is our job to teach all of our students (homeless or not) how to be kind and accepting.

Here is a list of books that can help classroom socialization and some suggestive follow up lessons:

Bully Trouble	By: Joanna Cole ISBN: 0394849493	Ask students to roll play ways they can avoid bullies and ask bullies to stop their mean behavior. Students can practice writing sentences with dialog about what they could say to a bully in the future.	Reading Level: 2.0
Blue Jay Girl	By: Sylvia Ross ISBN: 1597141275	The Blue Jay had the power to make a difference. Ask the class to think of other people in the world (may be from a previous history lesson) who have made a difference. Ask students to write about how they hope to make a difference someday (or today).	Reading Level: 2.0
Shelter Folks	By: Virginia L. Kroll ISBN: 0802851312	Ask students to explain why Joelle began to feel proud of her temporary home. Ask students to write about a place they have pride in (their school, home, car, playground, bedroom, shelter, grandma's house, etc.).	Reading Level: 3.4
Fly Away Home	By: Eve Bunting ISBN: 0395664152	In partners, have students compare and contrast life living in an airport vs. life living on the streets. After some discussion, assign each student a paragraph comparing the two.	Reading Level: 3.5
The Berenstain Bears Think of Those in Need	By: Stan Berenstain and Jan Berenstain ISBN: 9780679889571	Have the class make a list of items they need vs. items they don't need. Ask them to think of someone who may need the items that are extras.	Reading Level: 3.9
The Hundred Dresses	By: Eleanor Estes ISBN: 0152052607	Ask students to think and prepare a demonstration of their hidden talent. Once students present, ask each student to tell another student what they enjoyed about the presentation.	Reading Level: 5.4
The Queen Who Lost Her Castle	By: Johanna Carroll ISBN: 0595095631	Ask students to make a list of 5 attributes they love about themselves. Then, have students think of 5 students in the class who also have those attributes. Have students write a friendly letter to one of those five students thanking them for their good character.	Reading Level: 7.1

How I Do I Encourage Students To Work Together?

Guided Instruction

Throughout all guided instruction, provide students with the opportunity to discuss the new material. Remind students that they must speak one at a time and be good listeners. Create a variety or partners within student groups to encourage students to interact with others:

1. Shoulder Partners- next to each other
2. Eye Partners- in front of each other
3. Diagonal Partners- across from each other

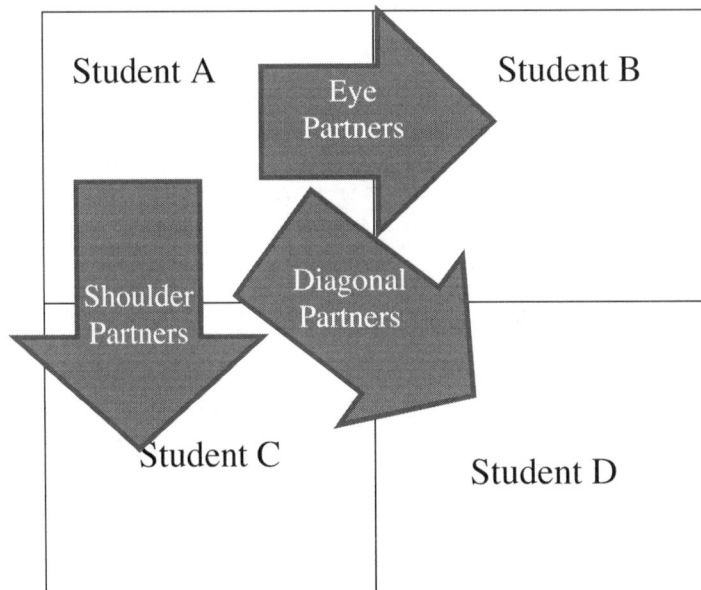

Provide students with a question or topic ("Tell your Shoulder Partner what you think photosynthesis is."). After allowing students to respond and listen to each other, ask "Who can tell me what their partner said?" This promotes good listening.

Cooperative Learning

When students are assigned to work in groups, assign roles within the group. This ensures that all students participate and work together, including your homeless student. Some roles could include:

1. Artist- Illustrates all work

2. Encourager- Keeps the other students focused and organized. This person also reminds students within the group to not interrupt one another so that everyone's ideas are shared. When students have completed a task, this student offers "high fives" or other forms of praise for success.

3. Note-Taker- Makes sure all written material is completed and turned in.

4. Discussion Leader- This person asks questions about how they group want to complete the task and poses questions to encourage deeper thought. This person also helps reminds students within the group to not interrupt one another so that everyone's ideas are shared.

5. Editor- Checks all work (throughout the work, not just at the end) and turns it in.

6. Vocabulary Enricher- Helps the group establish academic vocabulary and find synonyms for words they've used too frequently.

7. Time Keeper- This person makes sure all projects are completed on schedule and not too much time is spent on unnecessary items.

*Have these roles change each time you assign new group work. This ensures that every child has the opportunity to take on different leadership roles, which can help build self-esteem.

Academic Assistance

Let's face it, your homeless student is not in school every day and is often tardy, and misses a lot of lessons. So, what do you do?

Vocabulary- It probably hasn't taken you long to realize your homeless student has a very limited vocabulary. This can severely affect their reading comprehension and thus needs to be addressed quickly. Be sure to include a vocabulary lesson in your lesson plans daily. Also, (not just for primary classes) label everything in your class. Everything. Students may not have been exposed to telephones, light switches, computers, computer mice, clocks, sinks, etc. if they've lived in shelters, cars, or the street. By labeling everything around the room, students have a higher chance of developing vocabulary.

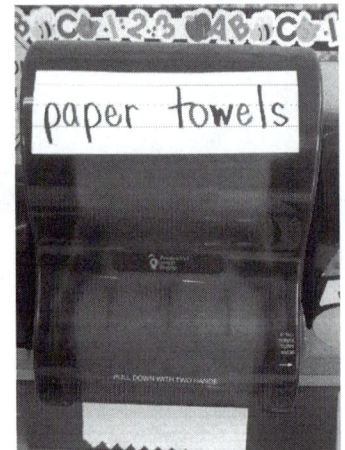

Small Group Instruction

Yes, our days are busy, but we can do it! During Silent Reading Time or Journal Writing, call a small group to a stationed area (same place every day for continuity) to work on a specific area of need. This mini-lesson doesn't need to be more than 5 minutes. Simply create one small goal, such as knowing to periods at the end of the sentence. Pull those few students who need help in this area and quickly cover it. You'll be surprised how effective those five minutes are when you have just three to 5 students. If this is done even only two days a week (the days the homeless student is at school) your student will not only academically improve, he/she will gain confidence, and a stronger relationship with you, the teacher.

Use Manipulatives

Numbers, symbols, geometric shapes, punctuation may have absolutely no meaning to a child with limited academic exposure. A plus sign may be confused with the letter t very easily and quickly confuse the student. Homeless students have a lot on their minds and need lessons to be fun and not too frustrating. Whenever possible, begin teaching a new lesson with manipulatives. A child may not understand symbols but he/she can understand things they hold, feel, and operate. Provide students with hands-on experiences daily. If your schools' materials are limited, make them. Card games, printed geoboards, beans, etc. can all be done cheaply and quickly.

After School Program

Chances are, your homeless student has missed a lot of school in previous grade levels as well and is far behind. If your school offers an after school program, such as "YMCA," or "Think Together," talk with the students' parents and your principal to make accommodations to enroll the student in these programs. Below are links for information about after school programs:
http://www.thinktogether.org/
http://www.ymca.net/
http://www.afterschoolalliance.org/
http://www.kaleidoscope-kids.org/programs

Tutoring

If you notice that your student needs more help than can be provided in a day's work, look into tutoring in the community. Many apartment complexes, shelters, and libraries offer free reading or math classes to young children. Your city should also have tutoring programs that are not free and donations can be collected to assist in these payments. If you're up for it, offer tutoring before or after school yourself as volunteer work. You being the tutor would be most beneficial because you already know the child's academic needs. Not to mention, it could help build your relationship with the student and homeless students need as many reliable adults in their lives as possible. Below are a few tutoring sites:

http://tutornext.com

http://info.connectionsacademy.com

http://aspses.com/

Computer Resources

There are millions of online educational games, tutorials, videos, articles, etc. for students to learn from outside of school. I know what you're thinking; these students probably don't have computer access or internet services. You're right they probably don't, but the library does and so does your school site. City libraries offer computer and internet use for free if the person holds a library card. Now a library card may be difficult to get without a permanent address but some libraries make exceptions. Your school site probably has a computer lab. What time does it open? What time does it close? Encourage students to come a little early to school or stay after a little longer to play these games, practice typing, or watch an educational video. If your computer lab closes early, talk to your principal to see if changes can be made to the schedule.

~~Home~~work

First of all, stop calling it <u>home</u>work and call it something else such as "independent practice" or "daily review." Calling it <u>home</u>work simply reinforces the student's lack of a home. Secondly, you've probably realized most, if any, homework is not turned in. Remember, many of these kids are doubled-up or living in shelters or on the streets. None of these places are really designed for quiet work. Accommodations must be made for the student. Ask the student what is limiting them from completing the work. Is their shelter/car/motel too noisy? Do they have a pencil or other needed materials at home? If the student is unable to concentrate because of the environment they are in, encourage the student to come early to school and complete it in the morning. If the student is lacking scissors, glue, pencils, or whatever is needed to complete the assignment you have two options: 1. Provide them with the needed materials (yes, ask for donations) 2. Change your assignment to better suit the materials the student has access to.

*Reminder, these are children are forced to act as adults as soon as the school bell rings. Please, do not take away recess or play time for not completing these after school assignments. They need as many opportunities to be children as possible.

Parent Communication

For many of us, when we need to communicate to a parent about a child's progress we call him/her. But what do we do if the parent doesn't have a phone? Most homeless adults do not have cell phones and if they do, they are the prepaid ones, which don't often last long. SO how do you reach the parent? First, try to meet the parent as soon as possible (before they drop the student off at school, at pick up, at the time of enrollment, etc.). On the following page there is a chart that suggests a variety of ways to communicate with the parent.

Communicating with Homeless Parents

Teach the parent how to set up a free e mail account such as Yahoo mail or Google mail. Arrange times that the parent can get access to a computer (such as at a library) so you know when they will receive the information.

Inform the parent that each day/week you will be sending home a note about progress, behavior, school dates, etc. so that every day, or particular week day the parent knows to look for the note.

Create a classroom webpage. Many teacher webpages even have an option for parents to privately logon and see their child's academic or behavioral status. Parents can check the website while at work, the library, a friend's house, etc.
(Jupitergrades.com, teacherweb.com)

Community Resources

Below is a list of organizations that can be helpful for you or your homeless student:

National Coalition for the Homeless	http://www.nationalhomeless.org/
Family Promise	http://www.familypromise.org/
United Way	http://liveunited.org/content/splash
Common Ground	http://www.commonground.org/
Homeless Shelters	http://www.homelessshelterssite.org/

References

Berliner, BethAnn. (2001) Imagine the Possibilities: Sourcebook for Educators
    Committed to the Educational Success of Students Experiencing Homelessness 2-205.

Bernstein, Nell., Foster, Lisa, (2008) Voices from the Street: A Survey of
    Homeless Youth by Their Peers 3-39.

Bronfenbrenner, U. (2005). Making human beings human: Bio-ecological
    perspectives on human development., 246-258.

Bruchey, Stuart. (1996) Children of Poverty: Studies on the Effects of Single
    Parenthood, the Feminization of Poverty, and Homelessness, 21-63.

Burt, M.R., Aron, L.Y., Lee, E., & Valente, J. (2001). Helping America's
    Homeless: Emergency Shelter or Affordable Housing? Washington,D.C.: Urban Institute. California
    Department of Education, 2010

Cunningham, M., Harwood, R., Hall, S. (2010) Residential Instability and the
    McKinney-Vento Homeless Children and Education Program: What We Know, Plus Gaps in Research,
    1-11.

Dood, John M., (1994) Evaluation Report, Parents and Preschoolers: An
    Intergenerational Literacy Project, 27-71.

FEANTSA, (2010) Ending Homelessness: A Handbook for Policy Makers

Hall, Ramona. (2007) Homeless Students and the Public School System

Hart-Shegos, Ellen. (1999) Homelessness and its Effects on Children, 2-13.

Herlin, L., Rudy, K. (1991) Homeless and in Need of Special Education, 7-34.

Hernandez Jozefowicz-Simbeni, (2006) Services to Homeless Students and
    Families: The McKinney-Vento Act and Its Implications for School Social Work Practice, 3.

Hindman, J., Stronge, J., Popp P. (2003) Students on the Move: Reaching Highly
    Mobile Children and Youth, 2-180.

Hombs, Mary Ellen. (2011). Homelessness: A Reference Guide, 1-299.

Israel, N., Jozeforwicz-Simbeni, D. (2006) Services to Homeless Students and
    Families: The McKinney-Vento Act and Its Implications for School Social Work Practice

Jackson, Terry. (2004) Homelessness and Students with Disabilities: Educational
    Rights and Challenges, 1-7.

Julianelle, Patricia. (2009). Using What We Know: Supporting the Education of
    Unaccompanied Homeless Youth, 481-525.

Kennington, P., Norris, J. (1992) Developing Literacy Programs for Homeless
    Adults, 1-115.

Levinson, David. Ross, Marcy (2007) Homelessness Handbook

Lovell, P. and Isaacs, J. (2008). The impact of the mortgage crisis on children, 1-5.

Miller, Andrew (2002) Mentoring students & young people: a handbook of effective
    Practices, 1-302.

National Coalition for the Homeless, McKinney-Vento Act, (2006)

Nord, M. (2009). Food insecurity in households with children: Prevalence, severity, and household characteristics, 1-44.

Nunez, Ralph. (2000) Homeless in America children's story

Marzano, Robert. (2003) What Works In Schools, 3-23.

Popp, Patricia, A., Stronge, James H., Hindman, Jennifer L. (2003) Students on the Move: Reaching and Teaching Highly Mobile Children and Youth, 5-170.

Reed-Victor, E., Stronge, J. (2000) Educating Homeless Students: Promising Practices

Samuels, J., Shinn, Ma., Buckner, J., (2010) Homeless Children: Update on Research Policy, Programs, and Opportunities

Shinn, Mary Beth. Rog, Debra., Culhane, Dennis (2005) Family Homelessness: Background Research Findings and Policy Options, 1-33.

Soyer, J. Guilbert, L. (1999) Give Us Your Poor: Homelessness & the United States: Teacher Handbook, 3-34.

Swick, K. (1999) Empowering homeless and transient children/families: An ecological framework for early childhood teachers. *Early Childhood Education Journal,* 23(3)

Swick, K. (2004). Empowering parents, families, schools, and communities during the early childhood years.

Swick, K. (2005). Helping homeless families overcome barriers to successful functioning. Early Childhood Education Journal, 33(3)

Swick, K. (2006). Families and educators together: Raising caring and peaceable children. Early Childhood Education Journal, 33(4)

Swick, K. (2007). Empower foster parents toward caring relations with their children. Early Childhood Education Journal, 34(6)

Swick, K., & Williams, R. (2006). An analysis of Bronfenbrenner's Bio-ecological perspective for early childhood educators: Implications for working with families experiencing stress. Early Childhood Education Journal, 33(5)

Swick, K., (2010) Responding to the voices of homeless preschool Children and their families, *Early Childhood Education Journal,* 38(4)

Torquati, J. C. & Gamble, W. C. (2001). Social resources and Psychosocial adaptation of homeless, school-aged children. Journal of Social Distress and the Homeless

Tower, Cynthia. White, Donna. (1989) Homeless Students

Vissing, Yvonne. (1996) Out of Sight, Out of Mind: homeless children and

Walker-Dalhouse, Dorris, Risjo, Victoria, J. (2008) Homelessness, Poverty, and Children's Literacy Development

Made in the USA
Middletown, DE
04 May 2015